THE LITTLE
PURPLE
POEM
BOOK

Aj Hill Yawn

Dedication

This book is dedicated to my family whom I love and adore with all of my heart! These are the people who inspire and give me purpose.

I want to dedicate my first poetry book specifically to my mother, Phyllis Vontress Yawn Hill. Thank you so much for all you have ever done for me despite your hardships. You raised me alone and were my village, helping me and my kids through everything possible.

I want to thank my Yawn and Hill family for all the love and laughter. I want to thank and dedicate this book to my grandmother, Corine Lyle, for her love and support and for showing me how close family should be and function.

I want to thank and dedicate this book to my father Archie Hill for passing his strength to me and always calling me his movie star actress since birth (he knew what no one else did), to my UX Designer husband, Derick Mcmullin for my graphics and his continued love and support, to my four beautiful children Millani, Paris, Royal, and Sir Pharoah who are my reasons for every move I make and every breath that I take (they keep me humble and grateful), to my brother Tirrell Hill for always looking up to me and pushing me to write this book, to my (Uncle/Daddy) Chief Petty Officer Douglas Yawn for being my father figure growing up, to my favorite Aunt Margie Yawn for my nickname at birth and always seeing the good in me when no one else did! To my handsome Uncle Jeffrey Yawn for giving me his charisma and wit, and always being a fun and funny light in my life. Rest in peace my uncles I love you.

To my favorite teacher, Mr. Calhoun, for always believing in me and giving me all the keys to unlocking my many artistic talents poetry, writing, modeling, and acting! I am forever grateful for you, my mentor.

In conclusion, I am who I am today because of all of you! I truly dedicate this book with all my love to each of you.

Love always your one and only AJ

TABLE OF CONTENTS

MY FIRST

The sky is clear
The moon is visible
This is it
This is the moment
When her brown eyes locked with mine
We just knew that it was time
As I lay back clenching the bed
Open wide
She calmly said
As I did
My legs began to quiver
I admit
I made some looks
This is nothing like the books
It's so intense
I am so nervous
She is doing a noble service
She tenderly placed her hands on my knees
While I yelled, "Oh Please!"
Reassured this is all normal
I lay back and try to relax
Let my body take control
And this woman play her role
I can no longer see her face
But she's inside my private place
Finally! The clear stuff came
As I screamed out her name
At last!
I feel such a warm rush
Followed by a heavy gush!
I am the wettest outside of a body of water I can be
The woman proudly lifted her head
And smiled
Congratulations on your very first child!

INTRODUCTION TO THE READER

Hello,
I hope "My First" duped you and made you smile. This
poem is just an icebreaker to get your mind thinking
outside of its norm. Now that you are acclimated and have
loosened up a little I hope that you are ready to embark on
this poetry journey that I have especially prepared for you.
Enjoy my heart, my soul, my experiences, my thoughts, my
perception, my opinion, my happiness, my sorrows, my love,
my laughter, my strength, and whatever pays the rent.

POET I AM

Poet, I is
Poet, I am
Poet, I be
Who really wants to listen to me?
Tiny little black girl from Cleveland, Ohio
Nobody ever clicks the link in my bio
Poet, I be
Poet, I am
Poet, I is
I grew up and had a couple of kids
Four to be exact
One girl and three boys
Doing my best to raise them with poise
Simultaneously, moved to Florida
My child got sick
But I took care of it
A little nervous, but became a reservist
Went back, grabbed my purse
Turned into a nurse
Now I'm a nurse with a purse
Poet, I be
Poet, I is
Poet, I am!
I grabbed that paper
And placed my stamp
I been a poet
Lil miss all know it
Whenever I speak it's my key
To unlock, who I am
My time to release
My inner beast
In order to keep the external peace!
I am a poet!

PURPLE ROSE BLOOM

Thy royalty
Thy majesty
Thy beauty tis unmatched
Tis amazing that thou art real and blooms natural
So delicate and elegant is each petal
Purple Rose
So unique and rare
Requiring such gentle and precious care
Tis a sweet aroma that fills the air
Smells so good!
Tis able to combine divine femininity and masculine energy
Beautiful rose petals are known to settle fights
And romance the night
Thy velvety petals are adorned
While thy elongated stem is strong with thorns

At last, thy innate protection from predators
Thou art a beautiful mix of red and blue
Attracts pollinators too
Purple rose bloom
Placed on caskets and death sites to mourn
A representation of the heart when tis torn
Purple rose
Oh, No! Thy withering bloom
Thou falleth underneath the moon
But with death comes regeneration
Rose petals get smaller in thy center
And lie dormant in the winter
In the morning, the sunshine will give its light
Thy rose will bloom again ever so bright
Each petal deserves a metal
Diverse in its existence
Bloom purple rose
Personify persistence

FINAL WISHES

These are your wishes
Ashes to ashes
Dust to dust
On the shelf hanging with us
Selfish wishes
Wish I could go to your gravesite
And whisk the earth up within you rest
Allowing it to softly flow through my hands
Hear the birds chirp
Like natures band
Experience the wind bend
A gust go by
So, I can feel your spirit fly
All the while sending reassuring chills through my body
I just want to lay on the land that your past vessel lies under
While viewing the fluffy clouds
And listening to the skies thunder
Rumbling out my heartache and pain
Perhaps there will be a chance of rain
On my skin, the drops will feel
As they did come from my eyes

When you left my humbled side
The refreshing smell will remind me of the comfort
I found in your scent
Oh, was it magnificent
If lightning strikes, I will not fear
I'll know the reflection of my anger is here
Perhaps the sun will reappear
Shine again
And remind me of your warmth
Imaginably
A harmless bug will settle upon me
Reflecting your gentle touch
May the sight of the flowers exemplify your beauty
While I look up to something strong above all
It's a tree
Reminding me to stand tall
With its leaves whispering to me
I'll hear you, mama
You are everywhere with me
Finally, I realize
Our final wishes are the same
But differently

WANDERING SOUL

I can feel my soul
I can feel that it's old
Can you feel this?
Temporary adherence to flesh
You can sense that it's only stationary until you rest
Every time I close my eyes
I can feel my soul rise
Above the rest
So, I ask?
While I slumber,
Does my spirit fight a spiritual war?
Does it witness violence and gore?
Am I at my happiest and free to wander?
Am I in heaven with my ancestors?
And when I wake
Can my soul come back possessed?
Or obsessed with the unknown?
Weaker or stronger against sin?
Walking in a disguise
UNBEKNOWNST amongst men
The soul and the flesh are intertwined
Only lasting for a short time
If my soul leaves while I sleep
I pray to the Lord
I come back as his sheep

…until we meet
For my soul was never mine
It will transform back someday
Or present in a different way
But at what price will I have to pay?
Until then,
I will cover my wandering soul
And my flesh growing old
With hopes of a better place than here
One without trauma, turmoil, and fear
My soul is forever!
It's my biggest jewel
And my greatest treasure
Condemn it? NEVER!
My soul is very clever
Because no matter what's done to this flesh
I live on forever!
Wander on my soul
When this body grows cold
At last, it's free!
No hold, not sold
Not bound, not lost
Free to wander where everyone will be
My energy is now a synergy
Where it is supposed to be
My wandering soul is happy

IMAGINE

Imagine someone to love and love you forever
Imagine little hands reaching out
Imagine endless love without a doubt
Imagine a heartbeat
Imagine the sound of little pattered feet
Imagine going insane but in the end
It was all worthwhile
Having something so precious as a newborn child
Imagine someone that calls you mommy
Imagine being a role model
To someone you once nursed or bottled
But did you ever imagine those sleepless nights?
Only periodically resting in the light
Imagine in return you get a baby that feels loved
And trusts in you
Imagine comforting your baby when they're sad and blue
Imagine!
Because that's about all I can do
This is the kind of pain that I never knew
The kind of pain your momma said
she never wanted for you
The birth of you is something I feared

Never imagined the terror of not having you here
To hold close
And to love on the most
I don't have to imagine a fetus inside
Or a great dent in my pride
I don't have to imagine the ultimate heartbreak
Or a surreal feeling I just can't shake
I don't have to imagine an ultrasound without a heartbeat
Or no movement
I don't have to imagine how nothing was soothing
Or how much I knew I was losing
I don't have to imagine how much I cried
For my baby that died
I just wish to imagine working hard to raising a star
That lives in a nice house driving a nice car
With a heart of gold and an even better soul
Raising a beautiful family while growing old
And me being able to say I did that day to day,
week to week, month by month, and year to year
I just wish I could imagine without tears
My baby that is here
Imagine that!

Written and dedicated to my baby, 2004

FRAGILE HEART

The heart beats steadily
Tha thump tha thump
The heart supplies the life
The heart breaks easily
The heart cries
It bleeds out
When the heart is happy
It fills up
And it beats
At its maximum capacity
Tha thump tha thump
Take care of the heart
And the heart will take care of you

DM's

DM'S

That boy in my DMs said I was Preeetty!
That boy in my DMs said I was Preeetty!
That boy in yo DMs ain't tell you he was sadiiiiTy
That boy in yo DMs ain't tell you he like all the kiiitty's
That boy in yo DMs ain't tell you he had 10 baby mamas
And 5 kiiiddies (Yeah! Keep up)
That boy in yo DMs ain't tell you he wore a wiiiig (just like yours)
That boy in yo DMs ain't tell you he smokes ciiii-igs (SquallAY's!!)
That boy in yo DMs ain't tell you he was abusive, possessive,
And in-truuusive!
That boy in yo DMs ain't tell you he was between jobs, had no car,
Would get you pregnant, and go to the baaar!!
That boy in yo DMs ain't tell you he lived far
And had no heeeeaRT!
That boy in yo DMs ain't tell you he was zeeea-lous
In being jeeea-lous

That boy in yo DMs ain't tell you he can't tell the truth
If his name was August Alsina at the red TAaaa-BLE!
That boy in yo DMs ain't tell you he was self-ish
And doing women hell-ish!
That boy in yo DMs ain't tell you he's not trustworthy
And out here doing women diiiir-ty! (protect yourself)
That boy in yo DMs ain't tell you he likes to dress like Bruce
Jen-ner while you're out getting DiiiinneR!
(Eat the stick up better than you)
That boy in yo DMs ain't tell you he had addiiiictions
That boy in yo DMs ain't tell you he had convictions
That boy in yo DMs ain't tell you he did a biiiiid
For touching all those Kiiiiids!
That boy in yo DMs ain't tell you that he ain't shiT!

ANONYMOUS

I don't know you
And you don't know me but…
If we were to exchange numbers
Then what?
If we were to talk and go out
What next?
If we were to hug and kiss
Would it turn passionate?
If we were to have sex
Would it turn into making love?
Who am I to you?
And who are you to me?
Should it be you and me?
How long will this last?
Do you expect it to be a roller coaster
Or a freaking blast?

Will I be happy or miserable?
Leader answer me!
This you must know?
Take a chance on a man?
I can already see you're un-confident in the plan
By the way that you stand
Well, let's go back to the beginning
When I was happy and winning
Before I didn't get your name
And played this foolish game
I never knew you
You never knew me
Remain anonymously
Funny thing
Future me randomly saw you again
But I will always remember what could've been
Now, I am so proud of the decision I made back then

IN THE END

I tried and tried again
To stop our love from coming to an end
But it did after I had your first kid
I knew I loved you so much after the first touch
And you know that I don't ask you for much
So, why do you continue to treat me this way?
I think about you every day
In every way
I thought you loved me as I loved you
But now, I see that wasn't true
Because now we're through
I thought you knew where I was coming from
And was through with acting dumb
See I have been mistreated by men my whole life
Feeling as if my heart has been stabbed by a knife
Whenever I looked into your eyes
It seemed you would never lie
Until the day came when you did me wrong
I surprised myself that I stayed with you so long

I always play the fool
Wind up sinking in a pool
Tired of this shit
You always messing with some chick
I give you my heart and you play games?
All I know is that I'm through messing with lames
I love you but I hate you
And this is something that will never change
But why is a part of me still wondering,
Will things ever be the same?
Do you see where this leaves me?
Sitting all alone with our baby at home
We aren't lovers or friends
Just unsuccessfully co-parenting
In the end
The cycle just begins!
We passed this unhealthy love to our child
That is something so selfish, unruly, and wild!
I'll NEVER forgive you!
I cried and cried again for you to love me till the end

LONELINESS

Is anyone there?
I am screaming in a void
It's quiet but loud
Lonely, but it is crowded
Several voices none mine

22

WHY DOES HE LOVE ME

Why does he love me?
Is he insane?
He must not know who I truly am
He must not know my name
What is it about me that caught his interest?
Could it be my hair?
It must be something there
Because I can tell by the way that he stares
Could it be my thighs?
No, it's something more by the twinkle in his eyes
Could it be my attitude?
Or the way my body feels in the nude
Why does he love me?
The more I push him away
The closer he will stay
He's so perfect!
I don't think I deserve it
It must be a trick!
I never get the good
Someone to treat me right
Someone to lay with me
And caress me till the middle of the night

Why does he love me?
Once knowing that I had feelings for another
Why do people love people?
Is a question I ask my mother
She said you can't help who you love
Just don't get it confused with lust
Love entails more than lust
You must also have trust
So, what is it about me?
Is there something he sees in my eyes?
He looks at me as if I bare some kind of surprise
But it's not that either
Because what's in his heart is something deeper
That will never tear us apart
His love for me is off the chart
He's so loving
He's so kind
And I'm still confused in my mind
What is love? Is the real question
But people can only give a suggestion
Behold, I see
Love is the true mystery
And when I figure out what love is for myself
I doubt I'll have to ask
Why does he love me?

HOPEFUL RICHES

I want to be rich
Anonymous my name
Because I don't want the fame
I want to be rich
Take my kids to the top
The grind in my blood
Won't let me stop
I want to be rich
I guess now that I think about it
I already am
Minus the glitz and the glam
I want to be richer!
Than the dude who wrote Green Eggs and Ham!
But one thing
Me and Sam are not the same
make sure to anonymous my name
is something I won't change
I want to be rich and that's it!

26

THE MEANING OF HOME

Man, I want a home
Somewhere I can call my own
Pick up the phone
Or just be left alone
Kick my feet up
Recline my seat
Eat me a feast
Comb my hair
Look around and see nobody there
Some place that is all mine
Some place I can unwind
Run around my backyard
And remind myself getting here was hard
But I reached for the stars
Played my cards
And I started living large

I will want to thank those who doubted me
For putting me right where I wanted to be
How do you like the nude me?
Because it's the new me
This is my Home!
A place where my body, my mind,
and my thoughts are free
Not a place I'm paid a fee to be me
The place where I undress and reveal the best
The best of me is what I see
My reflection is perfection
My home is someplace I can build, shape, and mold
Somewhere I can take control
And see myself growing old
Man, I want a home!
Somewhere that completes me
Someplace I can extend my family tree
I will build my home!

I REMEMBER THE FIRST DAY OF SCHOOL

I remember the first day of school
My momma told me don't go up there acting a fool
But what did I do?
I went up there and I cut up
Told the teacher to leave me alone and to shut up
That's when she said I'm calling your momma!
So, I laid down my head
Because when I get home
I just know that I'm dead
After, a long dreadful day of school
I walked into my house as timid as can be
I didn't see my momma anywhere
But then I turned a corner
And oh boy, was she there!
Dark and slender with a scarf on her hair
She was silent
Not a peep, not a scream, not a shout
She was quiet as an itty-bitty mouse
Hmm, Now I'm so scared and so terrified
I'm so confused
Because maybe I died
I started to manipulate and lie
Or maybe just run and hide
This day was torturous
I spent all day on eggshells
With my mind being a prison cell

My mom knows just what she's doing
Or maybe she's showing me some leniency
Because she actually sees me in her
But then again, she still hasn't said one word
Well, I'm going to sleep in my comfortable bed
And guess what?
I still have my good-looking head
I am finally in a deep sleep, so peaceful and calm
Dreaming a good dream of me a new mom
Splash! What is this?
An ice bomb?
It was cold water and ice!
And my momma wasn't nice
She calmly passed me a piece of paper
It was full of tasks and manual labor
Here, I am woken up in the middle of the night
Three AM to do the dishes on site!
To clean the walls and do the floors
I mean I did everybody's freaking chores!
This routine lasted all week
Every night I needed a new sheet
And at school, I was the coolest geek
And I never disrespect those who teach
But I must admit my mom was very clever
She taught me how to be quiet and move in silence
And even more so not to disobey her guidance
Yeah, I remember the first day of school

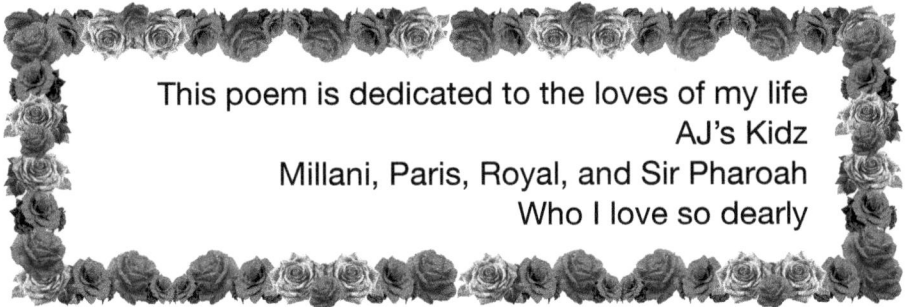

This poem is dedicated to the loves of my life
AJ's Kidz
Millani, Paris, Royal, and Sir Pharoah
Who I love so dearly

THE STORM

The sky is light blue
But rumbles thunder
The sun shines so bright
But flashes of light strike over yonder

WHY CAN'T I CRY ANYMORE

Why can't I cry anymore?
I used to cry all the time
From the bad memories that replay in my mind
I just can't cry anymore
Even though my heart is still sore
I cried in foster care
Because you said you'd be there
I cried when we were homeless
And I was hopeless
I cried when we were in a shelter
And because I felt sorry for the hand God dealt her
But I guess if you play your cards right
You'll live another good night
I cried from the permanent cut that I have
But I guess, that was all part of my path
I cried when you said you loved me and would change
But the next day things would still be the same
I cried when you said you would get out of that
abusive relationship

But another night, another sip, another hit
Would leave you feeling like shit
I cried when you pawned all our stuff
Just to get another puff
I cried Daddy when you went to jail
Leaving me to live in this hell
I cried my love when I asked you
To just spend time with me
But still, you rather run free
I cried my friend when I had to move away
I still miss seeing your face every day
I cried my brother when I left you to go through
what I've been through
I cry Mommy
Because I never know the day when you won't be
So lucky to come home and you'll leave us all alone
Is this how you love us by not putting us first?
This is a bad dream or even worse a curse
For attention and love, I turn to boys
Playing with them like little toys
Is this the kind of life you want for your child?
To be unruly and wild?

So much anger has built up inside
I could explode!
My heart has already become cold
I am too young for this!
Carrying the burdens of someone's hit
I'm supposed to be loved
Filled with happiness and sealed with a kiss
My eyes hurt from crying everyday
From believing every promise you made
I cannot cry anymore
My eyes are too sore
I can't cry! I can't do it!
Look on the list
I've probably already been through it

MY BIGGEST ENEMY

The world is against me
But I am the enemy
Drugs and alcohol are great friends to me
This makes no moral sense
You are the only one you're up against

ADDICTION

Alcohol, heroin, pills, crack, smoke addicted to dope
No one's perfect, nobody expects you to be a pope
But letting a substance overcome and take all of your hope
It's not the best way to manage and cope
Addiction is self-affliction
One of the world's biggest contradictions
Addiction is used to fix oneself
To be your savior?
To be your help?
It does nothing but mask what you've felt
Causes more scars and more welts
One must dig deep and leap into themselves
It's hard work to free yourself
But it's the most rewarding when you do
Then you can finally walk in your truth
Everyone asks how we got here
How do some get addicted for fun?
How do some do it out of repetition?
How do some do it, to repeat history?
But how we got here doesn't matter to me
How we turn them loose and set them free
Should be the only plea
Addiction has plagued my family tree
How many can say the same as me?
I'm pretty sure there's plenty

Listen to me!
For a long time, addiction tried to claim my brother
And that boy drank like no other
Doing anything just to mimic his mother
Addiction could be heard through my mama's cries
From the sexual abuse of those guys
It can be seen through my Auntie's eyes
Once they were bloodshot red
Waking every morning regretting every evil
Word that she said
Could've gotten pulled in myself
From all the pain and the hand that was dealt
This is generational
Minus the wealth
But operational destroy oneself
How can something be so strong and so powerful?
Cause all kinds of sin!
Kill you off, turn around, and manage to do it again!
Addiction wins!

We all hurt!
You are strong!
You are not alone!
If you have tomorrow
Tomorrow can always
be different!
RIP James Kimbrew

YOU VS I

You are ugly
I am beautiful!
You are lazy
I am a hard worker!
You are crazy
I am very sane!
You are nothing
I am everything!
You are not enough
I give my all!
You fall short
I am very tall!
You are weak
I am tough!
You don't have anything
I have the world! I have enough!
You look like a boy
But I am a girl!
You don't have any jewelry
I am the diamond and the pearl!
You show no restraint
Who are you to tell me I can't?!

You are always scared
I am fearless!
You don't have any hope
I have faith!
You always beg
I'd never, please!
You don't forgive
No, I never forget!
You are full of regret
I learned a lesson
So, this I'll accept!
You do not give to others
I give my all
You are not compassionate
Even more; I empathize
You are a liar
I tell my truth
You don't know who you are!
I do! I am You!
You are my biggest critic
My greatest analytic
They can't say anything to hurt me!
That, "YOU!" haven't already said
I am you, me, we, she, her, and us!
Inner you just hush!

FIGHTER

My bones are weak
My body aches
My smile is beautiful yet fake
I am a fighter

HAPPINESS

Boy, when I'm happy
Nothing in this world can get at me
The sun seems brighter
My smile spreads wider
The days seem shorter
But my excitement has no border
It is hard in this life
So, when you're happy through it
There is no depressed bottomless pit
The darkness never lasts too long
So, hold on be strong for a little bit
Remember day and night take turns
Smile, hold your head up, back straight,
And never make your happiness wait
So, I lead with my words
And proceed with my actions
Everything now is to my satisfaction
My heart is happy
My soul is joyful

HAPPY FACE

I am not happy
I smile, joke, and laugh a lot
But there are twists to the plot

THE PAST

I put the past behind me
But it continues to creep into the present
The present is now
The past becomes the future,
Then the future becomes the past
Save me from my past!
It hunts me at every walk of life
Past leave me alone!
Present change me!
Future save me!
Enough!

I do not want a past!
But without the past
There is no present
There is no future
There is no me
Past, present, and future interlink
Don't let me sink
Or drown in tomorrow
Engulfed in depression and great sorrow
Past be my strength
Present be my reflection
Future be my direction
Become one to form a better me

SINGLE MOTHER'S RUTH

You work hard like no other
You are shamed if you do
And blamed if you don't
Just because you do what others won't
Taking the place of you and your mate
Nobody chooses that fate
You are the good girl and the bad guy
Raising these kids, you secretly cry
Everyone's enemy until you die
Single-handedly raising these kids is a big bid
Sometimes your hard work won't even show
Because these kids now are so ungrateful
Looking for someone to blame
Someway to show out
Is the way they scream and pout
But you stay and you work it out
Because you are the strong one
Like you have no other choice but to be
Unlike your counterpart
You're like a rare work of art
You are there day-to-day
To pay the bills and fix the meals
Mama, you arrange the activities
And all the festivities
You take your pay, just to let them play
You do the laundry and the cleaning

And everything in between it
You are the taxi,
The psychologist
And the sitter
Everything but the quitter!
You do the teaching and the preaching
You are the mechanic and the nurse
Never putting, "You" first
Taking care of yourself with nothing left in the purse
A 24-hour job isn't even enough to do the job for two
Y'all don't hear me
Y'all have no clue
Y'all know nothing of a single mother's ruth!
Take a look at the Facebook
A single mother celebrating
Mother's and Father's Day got them shook
Turning into crooks
Writing Twitter books
Men and women are so bitter and passionate
It would be insane to try and ration it!
They need to take a look at their brethren
And with the same passion
Check them then!
Because where are the men?
Leaving all the women to fend
Y'all rather live in the lies than face the truth
Man, y'all know nothing of a single mother's ruth
Sick and all she still has to do what she do!
So, I'll say it, sis, "We appreciate YOU!"

WISER

My thoughts are strong
My mind is smart
My heart is broken
My eyes are tired
My breath is taken
I am wiser

UPLIFT ME

Hold your head up high
Shoulders back
Stand up straight
You are black!
There is no other race I'd rather be!
Inventive, creative, and courageous
Our style is contagious
Lips so full
Hips on drool
Breast to the East and to the West
More for him to fondle and caress!
I'm not mad at it!
Everybody else pays for that kit
Now, hold your head up high
You are fun, funny, with lots of wit
Nobody can put a finger on what makes you it
Smart, intelligent, spiritual
Double consciousness of the black soul
You require two fields of vision
That takes great precision
For the world to make a decision
On whom you are

When half the world isn't even up to par
Shoulders back
You are the prize! You are the gem!
Everything is earned never given on a whim
Black is beautiful
Your sashay is unique and bold
Compassionate, givers, with a smile of gold
Remember you once sang songs
Through the roughest rivers
Your history is proof you're worth-ful
Wagering, betting, and being sold
A hot commodity is what I see
You are what others wish to be
Afraid?
Because you are dangerous!
Stand up straight
When you're independent, resilient, motivated,
and hardworking
You will always find the devil lurking
So, pitch your pitch!
All my shades and all my colors
Now, walk with pride
Cause baby we outside

BLACK HAIR

This hair stubborn
Maybe she's Southern
She's so thick
Ain't nothing quick
Oh, that hair she's so beautiful
Black, brown, worn with a crown
Combing it sometimes can bring you a frown
She comes in many sizes, colors, and shapes
You can style her all the way to her nape
Sometimes she's so big
Folks think she's a wig
Hair so long, thin, short, loose, or tight
No need to cry everything will be alright
When you have the creatives on your side
There's no need to run and hide

Kinky, flowy, stiff
Whatever she is there's a style for it!
She can be...
Blown out, swing her wild
Braided down a thousand miles
An Afro, natural, or bedazzled
Spiky or in knots, she'll stay neat in one spot
Twisted out, bounce her about
Loc'd up, the skies the limit
For the shapes she can make
Worn straight, just give it a shake
Curled up, flip it out
Pinned up, sculpted high or low
They will ask to touch her wherever you go
Yes! Take pride in that hair
Be gentle, give her love and care
In any style that's chosen to wear
At last, embrace that beautiful black hair!

ENDANGERED TIGER

The world's biggest cat
One of the most endangered
Known for their great strength

BLACK WOMAN

It is the pep in her step
The sound of her heels
Her lips that are so full and thick
Every detail and bold feature of her face
Making anyone vulnerable to what she say
Strong, sophisticated black woman
Do you know where you've been?
Always silenced and second to men
Now she walks with her head held high
Knowing she's earned it through her ancestor's cry
Black woman!
Do you know your choices for being black?
You rarely make it, you rely on the system, you are ghetto,
A drunk, too dramatic, or a crack addict

But no!
Not these black women of today!
They don't allow anyone to stop them
Or to get in their way
Well, black woman why do you love this man so?
He wasn't worth it ya know
Between the disease and the baby
You could've been a bagless lady
Black woman!
It's ok you're stronger than you think
You deserve more than you know
Because everything about you is powerful
It is the pep in her step
The sound of her heels
Her lips that are so full and thick
Every detail and bold feature of her face
Making anyone vulnerable to what she say
That black woman is going to be ok!

THE BLACKER THE BERRY

They say the blacker the berry the sweeter the juice
I say the blacker the berry the sweeter the juice
The more they think you're loose
Not pretty enough
But is it true?
Not witty enough
Opting for those without a clue
Not the whole package to be your boo
Not successful enough, with something to lose
Not smart enough, to pick and choose
The black
The berry
The sweet
The juice
Oh, you're cute to be a dark skin girl
Baby, I'm a beautiful black one-of-a-kind pearl
See you underestimate me at all costs
It's never my failure but forever your loss
The black
The berry
The sweet
The juice
I can promise you
The sweeter his tooth
The more rewarding
I smile at the truth

The black
The berry
The sweet
The juice
Hide me in the shadows?
While you parade the cattle!
"You," living your truth is only half the battle
The black
The berry
The sweet
The juice
Y'all be adoring everything that's uncouth
Honestly, I don't even like how y'all move
TV and music obsessing with what's lighter than you
Growing up I just wish I knew what I knew
The black
The berry
The sweet
The juice
Loving myself
My melanated skin be glistening
While some of y'all be heavily conditioning
I need the world to be listening
Because I'm not going to address this again
The black
The berry
The sweet
The juice

How many can say they're sun-kissed?
Not sun-burned
It's my moment
It's my turn
To tell you about
The black
The berry
The sweet
The juice
The sun lets me know
I'm the chosen one
Young looking
With no DNA damage up under the sun
Everything about me is succulent
My brown skin is a big win
And if you ask me
I give it a 10!
The black
The berry
I'm sweet
And I got the juice!

CHAMPAWAT TIGER

Terrorized people
The deadliest of all time
Finally extinct
Once at the top of the chain
To shot down and being slain

I AM A PURPLE GIRL

I am a purple girl
Purple girls are the best in the world
Purple is royal
Purple is loyal
I am a purple girl
I love deep
Nothing over here is ever cheap
Purple is perplex
Purple is sex
I am a purple girl
I am exotic
Everything is sensual and erotic
I am a purple girl
Purple is a flower
Purple will advance you to devour
I am a purple girl
I am feminine
All the spice, sugar, and cinnamon
Purple is romance
Purple will have you dig deep
Shout out, "Here's your chance!"
Better be nothing shy of leaving me tranced

Wow! That purple girl is bold!
Nothing about her ever gets old

Because I am a purple girl!
I am rare
You reach my climax?
I wouldn't dare!
Purple is seduction
Purple is eruption
I am a purple girl
Nothing shy of magical
Stimulate my G-spot will get you a pot of molten gold
Purple is a mystery
Purple will keep you out of misery
I am a purple girl
I am to be personified
Take your time and make me feel glorified
I am a purple girl
Talk to me nice
Like when you want those sevens rolling dice
I am a purple girl
Touch me when you're gentle
And grip me tight when you're mental
OOOW! I am a purple girl
I love me a good eggplant
Make me say your name in a rhythmic chant
I am a purple girl

Purple is passion
Purple is fashion
Purple is never weak
Walk the runway so elegant and chic
I -AM -A- Purple-Girl
Purple is harmony, wisdom, and wealth
Purple is something never to be left
On a shelf like an elf
Purple is all so unique
Slide them panties to the side
Catch you a sneak peek
I am a purple girl
Purple is power
Purple is pride
You can't follow my walk or mimic my stride
Purple is a happy place
Leave you smiling with a happy face
I am a purple girl
Purple is peace
Purple is spiritual
Purple is enchanting and super lyrical

I am a purple girl
I right my wrongs
Sometimes with a smile
Sometimes with a thong

Man, this purple is all over the place!?
This purple sounds like a disgrace!

Don't be mad at me because I am a purple girl!
Purple is full of colors!
It's my truth, no need to fight!
Never said I was in black and white!
Just know my aura is something nice!
I am a purple girl
Judge yourself
I have nothing left for anything else
I am noble and of high status
I am cold, and I am the baddest!

I am a purple girl
A visionary and a creative
My presence alone is qualitative
I am a purple girl
A humanitarian
A good magistrate of character
I am magnificent
You'll pay just to whiff my scent
Well, of course!
A purple girl's soul searches for more
But she is never a revolving door
I am a purple girl
A burlesque mess
Playing me will be harder than chess
I am a purple girl
Take this warning and take heed
This is all of me
I take no sorry's or no plea's
But I do leave them asking
Who is SHE?!
I am a purple girl
And she is ME!

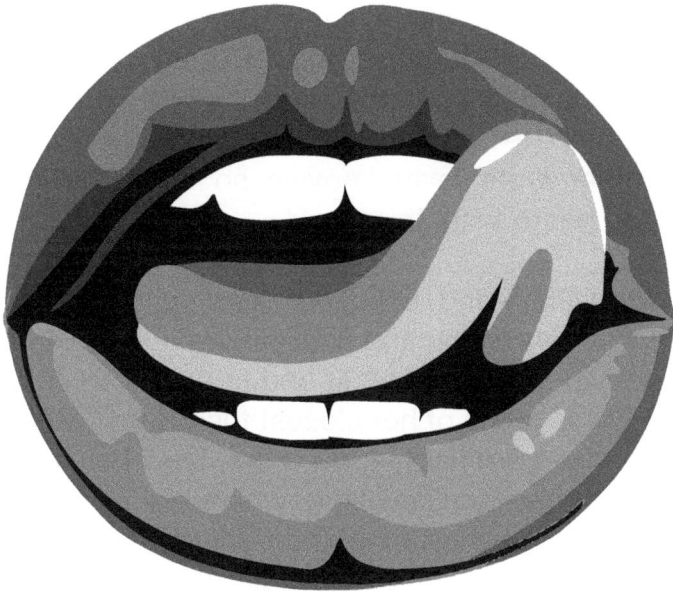

ABOUT THE AUTHOR

The author, Aj Hill Yawn, was born to Archie and Phyllis Hill. Aj has three siblings: two older sisters, Dameyon and Kimberly, and a younger brother, Tirrell Hill. Aj and Tirrell were always very close siblings who grew up in the same home together and took care of each other. Her little brother was always everywhere she went. Her brother wrote several novels, so it only makes sense that he encouraged her to write this book.

Aj is from Cleveland, Ohio, but grew up in Virginia and Florida. Aj had a very rough and challenging upbringing from the age of 5 years old after her mother and father divorced. Virginia is where she made some of her closest friends and received pertinent guidance from her friend's mom, Traci Paskins. As a teen, her family moved back to Cleveland, where she attended Shaw High School for a very short time, then transferred and graduated from Glenville High School in 2004. "Ville" is where Aj soared and explored all her artistic abilities guided by a great teacher and mentor named Cornelius Calhoun. This timeframe is where she wrote and performed poetry, performed in readings at Karamu, school plays, and much more.

In 2005, she gave birth to her first child, a beautiful and super-intelligent baby girl named Millani. After high school, she also attended Cuyahoga Community College, where she performed in Shakespeare's play *A Midsummer Night's Dream*. As a young adult, Aj reunited with a childhood neighbor and friend of the family, Chinetha Hall, who also saw beauty and an artistic light in her. Chinetha involved Aj in many modeling and acting opportunities. Aj modeled in East Cleveland's Fashion Show and Glenville Festival Fashion Show. Aj even modeled in the Jo Fleece Fashion Show in New York. Aj's early years were the prime of her modeling and acting ventures.

In 2007, Aj moved back to Florida, and two years later, she married her current and only loving husband, Derick. Her husband joined the armed forces, so once again, she had to move back to Virginia, and while she was there, she gave birth to her second child, a handsome and loving son named Paris. She also attended Tidewater Community College and obtained her first degree, an Associate of Science. Once her spouse's duty time was complete, they moved back to Florida. Aj went on to join the military as an Air Force Reservist and had two more handsome and charismatic sons, Royal and Sir Pharoah.

Aj devastatingly lost her beloved mother, Phyllis Hill, in 2020. This loss took a great toll and made a major impact on her life, but Aj continues to strive to make her mother proud. This poetry book was written and produced in honor of her mother's birthday. Happy Birthday!

During Aj's time in Florida, she has truly excelled. She has become a homeowner. Aj graduated from Rasmussen with an Associate of Science in Nursing degree and holds a Bachelor of Science in Nursing degree. She is currently a YouTube partner and can be found on the platform at Ajs1inatrillion. She is currently building a following on TikTok at Ajskidz. Aj would like to thank all her readers for their continued support, and she hopes everyone enjoys her poems as much as she did creating them.

9 798227 636003